Bibliographic information published by the German National Library:

The German National Library lists this publication in the National Bibliography; detailed bibliographic data are available on the Internet at http://dnb.dnb.de .

Imprint:

Copyright © 1978 GRIN Verlag
Print and binding: Books on Demand GmbH, Norderstedt Germany
ISBN: 9783346040398

This book at GRIN:

https://www.grin.com/document/501419

Volker Beckmann

The Etymology of OK

GRIN Verlag

GRIN - Your knowledge has value

Since its foundation in 1998, GRIN has specialized in publishing academic texts by students, college teachers and other academics as e-book and printed book. The website www.grin.com is an ideal platform for presenting term papers, final papers, scientific essays, dissertations and specialist books.

Visit us on the internet:

http://www.grin.com/

http://www.facebook.com/grincom

http://www.twitter.com/grin_com

The Etymology of „OK"

I   Dictionary Check-up

a) The Shorter Oxford English Dictionary on Historical Principles

"O.K. Orig. U.S.; initials of Old Kinderhook (near Albany), name of the birthplace of a Democratic candidate, Martin van Buren, used first as a slogan and passing into a term of approval, being interpreted as standing for *oll korrect* 'all correct'."[1]

b) Dictionary of Word Origins

"O.K. This symbol has probably more given sources than any other term. The favored seems to be Choktaw Indian *okeh*, it is so. Next comes the error due to bad spelling: *O.K.* marked on boxes to mean *All Correct*; this has been attributed to John Jacob Astor, and to President Andrew Jackson. There is also Obadiah Kelly, the early railroad clerk who initialed all parcels he accepted. And – to skip a dozen or more theories – there is the ME. word *hoacky*, *horkey*, the last load of a harvest. *It' s O.K. with me!*"[2]

c) The American Heritage Dictionary of the English Language

"O.K., OK, okay, n. pl. O.K.'s or OK's or okays. Also rare okeh. Informal. Approval; endorsement; agreement. - tr. v. O.K.'d or OK'd or okayed, O.K.'ing or OK'ing or okaying, O.K.'s or OK's or okays. To approve or endorse by signing with an O.K.; agree to. - interj. All correct; all right. Used to express approval or agreement. [Probably popularized by a slogan of the O.K. Club, the Democratic party's political club of 1840; for Old Kinderhook, the nickname of President Martin Van Buren, who was born at Kinderhook, New York; but previously attested in the 1830's as a modish slang abbreviation of favorable but uncertain meaning, possibly connected with another such abbreviation, D.K., for 'don't know'.] - O.K. adj. & adv."

"Usage:

O.K. (or OK) is especially appropriate to business correspondence and informal speech and writing, but usually inappropriate to expressly formal usage. In the following examples of general written usage, distinguished from the afore-mentioned, O.K. is termed most acceptable by the Usage Panel when employed as a noun (*his O.K. is considered a formality*, acceptable to 57 per cent)
or as a verb (*to O.K. an arrangement*, acceptable to 42 per cent).
As a predicative adjective (*all is not O.K. in their relationship*) it is
acceptable to only 23 per cent,
and as an adverb (*the radio was working O.K.*) to only 20 per cent.
Many Panel members term O.K. acceptable in speech generally, however."[3]

---

[1]   Little, W.; Fowler, H. W.; Coulson, J. (Bearb.); Onions, C. (Hrsg.): The Shorter Oxford English Dictionary on Historical Principles. Oxford 1973, Bd. II, S. 1442, 3. Spalte.

[2]   Shipley, J.T. (Bearb.), Dictionary of Word Origins. New York 1970, 2. Aufl., S. 250.

[3]   Morris, W. (Hrsg.): The American Heritage Dictionary of the English Language. Boston 1970, S. 914.

II   The Historical Background of OK

In the December, 1962 issue of the <u>American Speech</u>, A Quarterly of Linguistic Usage, Woodford A. Heflin wrote an article entitled "O.K. and its Incorrect Etymology".

In this article Heflin expresses heavy doubts about the theory saying that O.K.'s original meaning derives from "Old Kinderhook", the birthplace of the Democratic candidate, Martin van Buren. However, there is no question that the Democratic O.K. Club formed by radical supporters of van Buren really existed when a notice of a meeting of that club held on March 23, 1840 was entered in a Democratic newspaper called <u>The New Era</u>.

It was only a week later then that the Whig Party invented and published a story to discredit the Democrats. They said that Andrew Jackson, a famous Democrat in those days and a former President of the U.S.A., used the term for "Oll Korrect", all spelled with the letter "O" and correct with a "K". So the joke was aimed at Jackson's illiteracy.

In fact, there was some truth in the assumption that General Jackson could not spell correctly because he had not enjoyed a thorough education. "Jackson had merely attended a one-room country school house during his boyhood."[4]

During the presidential campaign of 1828, he was more than once attacked by men who had been educated at traditional English Universities. However, the fact that he made mistakes in his spelling turned out to be an advantage for his political career. The ordinary man sympathized with his failures and thus it was no surprise that he was elected President by an overwhelming majority in November 1828. But these linguistic deficits could not explain the reasons for his political victory. According to Arthur Schlesinger's "Urban Labor-Thesis" Jackson was primarily supported by the working men of the east coast, whereas Joseph Dorfman contended that Jackson was not primarily elected by the frontiersmen of the west or the farmers of the south but first of all by the businessmen and capitalists who profited from Jackson's decentralized and anti-monopolistic banking policies.[5]

Ironically, three men who had defended Jackson's misspellings in 1828 revived the story about the general's illiteracy during the political campaign of 1840. They

---

[4]   Cf. Allan Walker Read: Could Andrew Jackson Spell?, in: American Speech, Vol. 38, 1963, S. 188.
[5]   Cf. Gert Raeithel: Geschichte der Nordamerikanischen Kultur. Bd. 1. Vom Puritanismus bis zum Bürgerkrieg 1600-1860. Frankfurt a.M. 1995, 2. Aufl., S. 269.

intended to discredit the Democrats, especially the O.K. Club. If Jackson really used his O.K. for his pronunciation of oll korrect, it was hardly more than a phonetic joke.

Now the linguist Heflin assumed that the "all correct" meaning of O.K. had existed prior to the hot campaign of 1840. Both the Whigs and the Democrats claimed to have given O.K. the meaning of "all correct". The Whigs, who gave the term different meanings during the campaign, such as "Old Kalamity", "Old Klothes" or "Out of Kash" ended up with the "Oll Korrect" interpretation referring to Andrew Jackson. The Democrats presented the "Old Kinderhook" version. They also insisted on having adopted the "all correct" meaning as their own, although they could not accept the story about Jackson.

Whichever party might have been right or wrong, for Heflin the time of the political campaign was far too artificial and contrived to explain the emergence of the "all correct" meaning of O.K.

Instead, Heflin offered an alternative in his article. He referred to the study of Robert G. Gunderson which Ralph T. Eubanks also mentioned in his article "The Basic Derivation of O.K." In 1957 Gunderson found out that the term O.K. meaning "all correct" had been used in the Baltimore Sun which appeared on February 24, 1840. That point of time antedates March 23, 1840, the day the Old Kinderhook theory was related to by a full month. Thus the date shows that the "Old Kinderhook"-theory cannot explain the original meaning of O.K. Secondly, the date proves that the Whigs did not invent the "all correct" sense of O.K. on March 30, 1840.

Gunderson's citation referred to a story reporting that some friends had lost a julep to the editor of the New Orleans Sun in a bet. The last sentence read: "We hope that this (the julep) will satisfy him, and that he will give us acknowledgement that it is O.K."

Heflin found yet another piece of evidence in the Philadelphia Gazette which appeared on November 12, 1839. The editor of the Gazette had gone on a tour to New York and reported back the following observation:

"They have a curious, short-hand phraseology in Wall Street which it is amusing to hear. A man offers another a note with the endorsement of a third, - and saying of it – 'You see, it's A. 1, the man is decidedly O.F.M.'

'Yes – that's good – O.K. – I.S.B.D.'

'Will you make the contract we spoke of yesterday?' says the fourth person to a fifth, - 'I have brought my friend as witness.'

'Yes – we'll close it to-morrow.'

'A.R., - N.S.M.J.' is the reply: and the parties bow and separate.

The glossary to the foregoing is thus:

O.F.M. = our first man; O.K.= all correct: - I.S.B.D.= it shall be done; A.R.N.S.M.J. = all right, nough said among gentlemen, and so forth. This tongue-relieving process is quite in vogue here – it saves the common enemy, and is considered extremely useful."

So Heflin proved that O.K. was part of the American language used by brokers, bankers and businessmen at the end of the year 1839. Concerning business abbreviations Heflin also referred to D.K. which he believed to mean "don't know", although the linguist Mencken offered a different interpretation saying that the acronym meant the opposite of "all correct".[6]

In his 1962 report Heflin drew four conclusions:

1. The Old Kinderhook theory cannot explain the original meaning of O.K. because the term could be found in at least two newspapers articles which had been published before the radical club of the Locofocos was founded. The meaning of O.K. mentioned in the non-political and non-business area meant "good" and "all right" but not "all correct".

2. The history and the original meaning of O.K. remained unsolved.

3. The author assumed that the expression was widely known in 1839 and used early 1840 by the Wall Street and more generally by people who read newspapers, especially the <u>Baltimore Sun</u> and the <u>Philadelphia Gazette</u>.

4. The author speculated that O.K. had already lost its original meaning of "all correct" when used during the political campaign of 1840. This statement does not sound plausible because he mentioned above that the history of O.K. was still unresolved at the time of his research. Heflin, however, referred to examples showing that the meaning of the term O.K. changed at least twice within two years. Depending on the specific area – whether it was used in speeches or articles during the political campaign in 1840, whether in Wall

---

[6] Vgl. H. L. Mencken: The American Language, Supplement I, 1966, S. 278.

Street language or simply in a private report, O.K. was interpreted differently. Concerning the multiplicity of interpretations, the political campaign of 1840 seemed to foster a word-producing climate. The interpretations ranged from the Old Kinderhook theory to the reversal K.O. used by the Whigs who wanted the Democrats to be "kicked out" or perhaps even to be "knocked out".

Another author who thoroughly worked out the conditions of the development of O.K. is Allan Walker Read. In the February issue of the <u>American Speech</u> published in 1963 Read started a series of three articles, the first entitled "The First Stages in the History of O.K."
In this article the author supplies his readers with a great number of quotations and citations mostly taken from papers which appeared in the late 1830ies. By doing so, Read shows that the habit of using and inventing abbreviations, coinages and puns was very common at that time. Thus he describes the setting in which O.K. was very likely to emerge.

First, he presents the abbreviations "O.F.M." meaning "Our first Men", which Heflin mentioned above, and "W." meaning "Women".
Example: "A delightful little song written by J. T. Fields, one of our young Boston poets, … made quite a stir among our O.F.M., and W., too". (<u>Boston Morning Post</u>, July 23, 1839, pp. 2-3)
A forerunner of O.K. is n.g. standing for "no go" which means "impossible". Originally, n.g. was an English term and was chiefly used predicatively.
Example: "Then they went together to the plaintiff's to try to settle, but it was n.g." (<u>Boston Morning Post</u>, June 25, 1838, pp. 2-3)

Especially newspaper critics made use of abbreviations which sometimes were reduced to a single letter. "S" stood for "shocking", "m" for "mush".
Example: "The N.Y. Mirror's notice of Cooper's review of Lockhart's life of Scott is m. (mush)."
When some of the big colleges allowed young ladies to study for a certain degree called M.P.L. which meant "Mistress of polite Literature", a critic ironically recommended some alternative degrees, such as M.P.M. ("Mistress of Pudding

Making"), M.D.N. ("Mistress of Darning Needle"), M.S.B. ("Mistress of Scrubbing Brush") and M.C.S. ("Mistress of Common Sense").

Names of groups and societies were often abbreviated during the 19th century as well as today. So there is hardly any difficulty guessing what Y.M.S.F.M.T.C.O.T.I. meant. It was of course the "Young Men's Society for Meliorating the Conditions of the Indians".

But besides those oddities, the more important habit of abbreviating the names of alcoholic drinks has to be mentioned with reference to O.K. Read speculated that the situation when someone went into a bar and called out "M.J." which meant "mint julep" was quite realistic. The bartender who knew the regular customer very well could easily reply "O.K." Other acronyms invented for alcoholic drinks were O.D.V. which stood for the French word eau-de-vie or W.B. which meant "wine bitters".

As a good example to illustrate the craze for misspelling, the funny letters written by George W. Arnold (1783-1838) under the pen name of "Joe Strickland" may be referred to. Arnold spiced his letters with a lot of slang expressions and deliberately misspelled most of the words and thus succeeded in amusing his readers.

Another humorous kind of literature may be added. It is the sample from a poem entitled "To Miss Cathrine Jay of Utica". The Columbia Spy reprinted it July 21, 1832, p. 285/2.

> Still KTJ is far B4
> All other maides IC;
> Her XLNC I adore
> As a lovely NTT.

What Read wanted to say in this article is that the history of O.K. cannot be seen separately. The role of O.K. plays only a smaller part of the tradition of abbreviating words. As this tradition had existed long before the political campaign started in 1840, Read's findings are not surprising. They prove that in Boston a group called "Anti-Bell-Ringing-Society", O.K. meaning "all correct" became current as early as in the spring of 1839.

So both Read and Heflin have found out that originally O.K. meaning "all correct" did not emerge during the political campaign, but had been known to a limited number of people at least one year earlier. Yet the campaign of 1840 helped to make O.K. popular to a larger audience because each party appropriated O.K. and tried to make political capital out of it.

The campaign must have been really tough and quite modern in those days. It was the Whig's chance to beat the Democrats. The machinery of rhetoric and counter-rhetoric was set into motion, personal attacks were launched, newspaper headlines, mottos and slogans created. The Old Kinderhook theory emerged, the old story about General Jackson's not knowing how to spell was printed once again. However, O.K. meaning "all correct" occurred in those days, too. During the campaign, Blarney, a member of the Democratic party shouted in a speech, "Dear People! ... You are always right as a book, and nobody can gum you. In short, you are O.K."

After the election Democratic rule abruptly came to an end. The Whig candidate, General Harrison, was elected president. Harrison was said to lead a simple, modest life. Whig editors made the potential voter, the common man, believe that Harrison used to live in a log cabin and liked to drink hard cider. Whether true or not, at the end of the "Log Cabin Campaign" the image of the common man had shown its effectiveness. When addressing the electorate after the election, Blarney said in disappointment, "You miserable, despicable, know-nothing, good-for-nothing rascals!... Gummed by coon-skins! ... Dead drunk on cider! ... Go to the devil!..." (Frankfort, Ky., Commonwealth, October 20, 1840, p. 257)

In addition to the "Log Cabin Campaign", the Civil War, World Wars I and II influenced the expansion and popularisation of O.K. Famous men like President Wilson and Prime Minister Churchill used the term and gave prestige to the ordinary O.K. American troops brought the term to countries as far away as Burma and Japan. A general statement made by Thomas Pyles is interesting: "OK is, if anything, of more frequent occurrence nowadays in England (perhaps in Germany too, author) than in the land of its birth, ..."[7]

---

[7] Thomas Pyles: The Origins and Development of the English Language. New York 1971, 2. Aufl., S. 242.

Literaturverzeichnis

Zeitschriftenartikel

Ralph T. Eubanks: The Basic Derivation of OK, in: American Speech, Vol. 35, 1960, pp. 188-192.

Woodford A. Heflin: OK and its Incorrect Etymology, in: American Speech, Vol. 37, 1962, pp. 243-248.

Allan Walker Read: The First Stage in the History of OK, in: American Speech, Vol. 38, 1963, pp. 5-27.

Allan Walker Read: The Second Stage in the History of OK, in: American Speech, Vol. 38, 1963, pp. 83-102.

Allan Walker Read: Could Andrew Jackson Spell?, in: American Speech, Vol 38, 1963, pp. 188-195.

Allan Walker Read: Later Stages in the History of OK, in: American Speech, Vol. 39, 1964, pp. 83-101.

Lexika

Little, W.; Fowler, H. W.; Coulson, J. (Bearb.); Onions, C. (Hrsg.): The Shorter Oxford English Dictionary on Historical Principles. Oxford 1973, Bd. II, S. 1442, 3. Spalte.

H. L. Mencken: The American Language. An inquiry into the development of English in the United States. London 1966, Supplement I, p. 278.

Morris, W. (Hrsg.): The American Heritage Dictionary of the English Language. Boston 1970, S. 914.

Shipley, J.T. (Bearb.), Dictionary of Word Origins. New York 1970, 2. Aufl., S. 250.

Monografie

Thomas Pyles: The Origins and Development of the English Language. New York 1971, 2. Aufl., S. 242.

Kulturgeschichte

Gert Raeithel: Geschichte der Nordamerikanischen Kultur. Bd. 1. Vom Puritanismus bis zum Bürgerkrieg 1600-1860. Frankfurt a.M. 1995, 2. Aufl.